A YOUNG MAN IN GOD'S PLAN

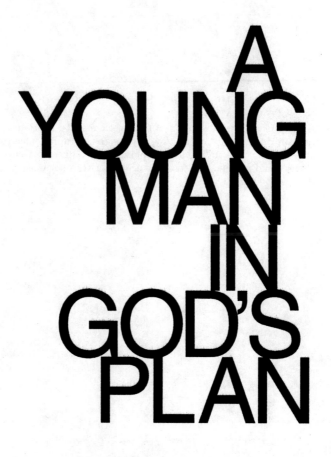

WITNESS LEE

Living Stream Ministry
Anaheim, CA • www.lsm.org

First Edition, November 1986.

ISBN 0-87083-264-6

Published by

Living Stream Ministry
2431 W. La Palma Ave., Anaheim, CA 92801 U.S.A.
P. O. Box 2121, Anaheim, CA 92814 U.S.A.

Printed in the United States of America

04   05   06   07   08   09   /   12   11   10   9   8   7   6   5

CONTENTS

PREFACE

This little book is composed of four messages given by
Brother Witness Lee in the spring of 1964 in Los Angeles,
California.

CHAPTER ONE

A YOUNG MAN IN GOD'S PLAN

Saul of Tarsus was a young man in God's plan. He was a young man called by the Lord according to the Lord's plan and for the Lord's purpose. Acts 7:58 tells us that "the witnesses laid down their garments at the feet of a young man called Saul." Then in Galatians 1:14 Paul tells us that he advanced in Judaism beyond many contemporaries in his race. "Contemporaries" refers to those of Saul's own age.

MAN—THE CENTER OF GOD'S PLAN

Our God, who is full of wisdom, has a plan, and the entire universe was created according to His purpose, His will, His plan. We must know what God's eternal plan is. In the next chapter we will see more concerning this. Man's position, man's place, in God's plan is very central. It is absolutely right to say that the Bible is a book full of Christ, yet we can also say that the Bible is a book full of men. Even God Himself became a man (John 1:1, 14). Jesus is the complete God and the perfect man. Even after His resurrection and ascension, He is still a man. Before Stephen was stoned, he said that he saw "the heavens opened up and the Son of Man standing at the right hand of God" (Acts 7:56). Stephen saw the Lord Jesus as the Son of Man in the heavens. Man is the center of God's plan. A bicycle wheel may have a hub with many spokes. The hub and the spokes subsist in the wheel. If the hub, the center, is taken away, the spokes will collapse. In like manner, without man as the center, God's plan would collapse.

GOD CALLING YOUNG PEOPLE
TO TURN THE AGE

We must also see that all the persons who were called by God to carry out His up-to-date move were young men. This does not mean that God would not use an older person or that God does not love the older ones. But the Scriptures reveal that all the persons who were called by God were young ones. You may think that Moses was called by God when he was eighty years old. But you have to realize that Moses had something divine working within him even before he was forty. From his very youth, he had something to do with God. When he was eighty, that was not the first time God came to him. God came to him when he was young (Acts 7:20-29). You may point out that Abraham was seventy-five years old when he was called by God (Gen. 12:1-4). But if you read the Scriptures carefully, you will see that Abraham was seventy-five years old when his father Terah died in Haran (Gen. 11:32). Acts 7:2 tells us that "the God of glory appeared to our father Abraham when he was in Mesopotamia, before he dwelt in Haran." The first time God called Abraham was while his father was still alive, and the second call came after his father had died. Therefore, the first time God came to Abraham was quite earlier than when he was seventy-five years of age. On the other hand, we have to realize that at Abraham's time, a man who was seventy-five years old was still quite young. I would not say that God would never call an older person, but the Bible and church history show that most of the time God has a new move with young people.

God calls young people to carry out His move because, generally speaking, young people are not set, settled, or occupied. With an older person everything is usually set. It is rather hard for him to have a change within. Also, everything tends to be settled with an older person. It is not easy for him to move on with the Lord. Also, older people tend to be occupied by many things. God would not call those who are set, settled, and occupied because whenever He calls a person that means He has something new to do. He calls someone because He has a desire to turn the age, to do something new and revolutionary.

From the time of creation God has always been going on. He has a plan, and with this plan He has an aim, a goal. In order to reach this goal He has to go on and on. With every step of the Lord's going on, there is always something new. With people like Adam, Abel, Noah, Abraham, Moses, and David there was always a new step of the Lord's going on. It is hard for God to go on with older ones because they tend to be set, settled, and occupied. It is much easier for God to do something revolutionary with young people, to turn the age from one direction to another direction.

Do you think that God is satisfied with the present situation of Christianity? Do you not think that the present religious system is something too old? Do you not believe that God is waiting for a chance to do something new, to have a change, to have a transfer, to have a turn in the age? The record of the Scriptures shows us many changes. There was a change in history with Noah, with Abraham, with Moses, with David, and with Isaiah. Then there was a great change, a great turn with John the Baptist. Finally the greatest turn, the greatest change, in the history of mankind was brought in by a young man named Jesus when He was thirty years old. Then the Lord proceeded to go on further in His heavenly ministry with the apostles.

Throughout the history of the church we can see how the Lord raised up young men to turn the age. The Lord raised up Martin Luther during the reformation to bring mankind out of the dark ages. This was a transfer in the age. God is always doing something new. He is always going on. Generally speaking, God does not impart something new through the aged persons, but always through young persons. Martin Luther was young when he was called and dealt with by the Lord. Zinzendorf was a young man when he was caught by the Lord as was John Nelson Darby, the leader of the Brethren assemblies. John Wesley, Charles Wesley, and George Whitefield were also young men when they were called by the Lord. Missionaries that the Lord used in church history to gospelize the world, such as Hudson Taylor, William Carey, and David Livingstone, were called by the Lord when they were young.

It is hard to find a case from the Scriptures or from church history where God called an older person to do something for Him in a new way. This is because every piece of God's work is something new. God is always going on, so He always needs a new start with a new nature in a new way and for a new age. Man is so central in God's plan, yet man must be used by God while he is still young. When you become old, the time for God's calling, the time for God's use, mostly is over. I do not mean that the time for God's salvation is over. Many older persons have been saved by God, but the time for God's use is mostly over.

KEEPING OURSELVES EMPTY, OPEN, FRESH, NEW, LIVING, AND YOUNG WITH THE LORD

The first young man used by God in the Scriptures was Adam. God did not create an old man. The word "old" came from the fall. If man had never fallen, he could never be old. If man had never fallen, it would have been possible for him to live many years and not become old. God had no intention to have many old men. God's intention is to have many young men with every one fresh, new, and living. None of us should be old. To be old means to be set, settled, and occupied. Sometimes some of the saints would refer to me as an old brother. It seems that this is a respect to me, but actually I do not like to hear this. I do not look upon myself as an old brother. I am not set, settled, and occupied. We always need to exercise to be young, to be new, to be renewed, to be fresh, and to be living all day long. It is only when you are young that there is a possibility for God to come in to call you, to choose you, and to use you to do something new. We need to give the Lord the way to go on in His progressive move through us. I hope that you will be a living, fresh, and new channel for the Lord to go on in His own way. This will require you to offer yourself to Him, to cooperate with Him.

When D. L. Moody was a young man, he heard someone say that something wonderful would be worked out on this earth if a man would offer himself fully to God, to be fully possessed and occupied by God. When he heard that word, he immediately responded to it. He gave himself fully to the Lord. That was the secret as to why God could use D. L. Moody so much and why the Lord could go on quite a distance of His way through D. L. Moody. I hope that we would take this fellowship and tell the Lord, "Lord, I thank You that I am still young. I do not want there to be anything set, settled, or occupied with me. I want to be fully open to You for Your new move on this earth. Lord, I give myself to You. Come in and occupy, take, and possess me for Your up-to-date move on this earth." If we would pray to the Lord in this way, we will be the persons who will turn, who will transfer, the age.

There is always something new to be worked out by God. The Holy Spirit is now working and moving in the hearts of the children of God for the carrying out of His move. He is ready, but He is waiting for some people to cooperate with Him. The situation in today's religion cannot satisfy God. God wants to do something new. He wants to do some-thing new in life, in knowing Christ, in experiencing Christ, in preaching Christ, in dispensing Christ, and in expressing Christ. The doctrines, the forms, the organization, the rituals, the regulations of organized religion, and the miraculous gifts cannot satisfy God nor can they fulfill His purpose. These are not what God's heart's desire is. God wants to do something new. He desires that Christ Himself would be known, realized, experienced, and expressed in a full and living way. If you are occupied with the miraculous gifts or with Bible knowledge, God cannot come in to use you for His up-to-date move. If you are settled into a certain form, organization, or ritual, you cannot be used by the Lord to fulfill His purpose. You have to be new, empty, and open, telling the Lord that you are here for nothing on this earth but for Himself. We need to tell the Lord that we are not here for religion, nor are we focused on teachings, doctrines, or gifts. But we are here one hundred percent for Christ Himself as the living One.

If you would be so fresh, young, and new with the Lord, He would have a way to carry out His new move through you. This is why the Lord said in Luke 18:17, "Truly I tell you, whoever does not receive the kingdom of God like a little child shall by no means enter into it." A little child, not filled with and occupied by old concepts, can easily receive a new thought. Hence, people need to receive the kingdom of God as a new thing, with an unoccupied heart, like a little child. You may be an older brother in years, and yet still be young in the spirit because you are not set, settled, or occupied. Whenever we open ourselves absolutely to the Lord, He has a way to dispense something new, fresh, and real of Himself, of His thought and desire, into our being. May the Lord gain a group of people in these days to turn the age for His new move.

If I could help others to be saved and to be raised up to love the Lord, to seek after the Lord, this would make me happy. But I would not really be satisfied until I knew that a good number of saints could be used by the Lord in His hand to turn the age through their life and work. We are not merely fellowshipping concerning salvation or spirituality, but we are dealing with God's eternal purpose. The young people need to realize that this is their golden time to be used by the Lord. The Lord needs you as a channel through which He can carry out His move. The way for you to grasp this opportunity is to go to the Lord to open and empty yourself. You need to give yourself to Him and allow Him to take you, to possess you. Never have something within your being set, settled, or occupied. Keep yourself empty, open, fresh, new, living, and young with the Lord. Then the Lord will be able to go on through you in a marvelous way. We all need to consecrate ourselves once again to the Lord for His eternal purpose.

CHAPTER TWO

SAUL'S BIRTH AND RELIGION

In the first chapter, we saw that Paul was a young man in God's plan. Paul became the very instrument, the very vessel, God used to carry out what was on His heart. As Christians, we also need to be persons in God's plan, so we first need to see what God's plan is.

THE HEAVENLY VISION OF GOD'S PLAN

Acts 9:1 tells us that Saul was "breathing threatening and murder against the disciples of the Lord." The Holy Spirit uses the word "breathing" to express what was in this young man. He did not merely threaten the disciples outwardly, but his persecution of the Christians was something from within him. His entire being was in it. When you do something and your entire being is in it, that very thing becomes your breathing. Acts 9:1 does not say that Saul was breathing threatening and murder against Jesus Christ but against the disciples of the Lord, against the Christians. Saul "went to the high priest" (9:1) to get the authority to persecute the disciples even more. While he was on the way to Damascus, the Lord intervened and revealed Himself to this young man.

"And as he went, it came about that he drew near to Damascus; and suddenly a light from heaven shone around him; and he fell on the ground and heard a voice saying to him, Saul, Saul, why are you persecuting Me? And he said, Who are You, Lord? And He said, I am Jesus, whom you are persecuting" (vv. 3-5). Although Saul was a young, strong man, the light from heaven caused him to fall to the ground. The Lord also told Saul, "It is hard for you to kick against the goads" (26:14). A goad is something that pricks, like a pointed rod used to urge on an animal. By this word, the Lord let Saul know that He was the Master and that Saul was in His hand and under His yoke. When an ox is not obedient, his master will use a goad to urge him on. Many times the ox will kick against this goad. The Lord let Saul know that he was persecuting his Lord, his Master, the very One who controlled him.

The voice did not say, "Saul, Saul, why are you persecuting My disciples, My followers, My believers?" But the voice said, "Why are you persecuting *Me?*" In Saul's realization he was persecuting the followers of Christ, the disciples. He never thought that he was doing something against Christ Himself, that he was persecuting Jesus. No doubt, Saul was puzzled by the question—"Why are you persecuting Me?" Thus, he asked, "Who are You, Lord?" (9:5). Saul called Him Lord because the voice had its source in the heavens. "Lord" here equals the word "Jehovah" in Hebrew. He recognized that this was the Lord who is in heaven, yet he must have wondered how he could persecute someone in the heavens, when he actually persecuted persons on this earth. The Lord answered Saul's question by saying, "I am Jesus, whom you are persecuting" (v. 5).

On the very day that the Lord Jesus met this young man, He gave Saul a clear vision that He is one with all His believers, that all His believers are one with Him. When you touch the believers, you touch Jesus. When you persecute them, you persecute Christ because they are one with Christ and they are Christ (1 Cor. 12:12). If the disciples, the followers, the believers of Christ, are not united with Christ as one, and they are not Christ Himself, how could Christ ask Saul, "Why are you persecuting Me?" It was as if the Lord were saying to Saul, "You have to realize that I, Jesus Christ, am one with My disciples. I am the Head; they are the Body. I and they are one person, one man." To Saul this was a unique revelation in the entire universe! By this he began to see that the Lord Jesus and His believers are one great person—the wonderful "Me." This must have impressed and affected him for his future ministry concerning Christ and the church as the great mystery of God (Eph. 5:32), and laid a solid foundation for his unique ministry.

Galatians 1:15-16a says, "But when it pleased God, who set me apart from my mother's womb and called me through His grace, to reveal His Son in me." These verses show us that God did not separate us from our school or from our job but from our mother's womb. This means that the Lord had separated Saul even before his birth. We also were separated before our birth and called one day through His grace. Perhaps after we had done many foolish things, after we had done much kicking against the goads, the Lord called us by His grace to reveal His Son in us. It is a marvelous fact that "it pleased God...to reveal His Son in me." Saul was greatly involved with the Jewish religion, yet God revealed Christ in him. He was busy with many outward things, yet God revealed Christ inwardly to him.

God's revealing of His Son to us is in us, not outwardly but inwardly, not by an outward vision but by an inward seeing. This is not an objective revelation but a subjective one. Christ revealed in us is the center of God's plan. God's plan is not to have a religion nor to have many religious works accomplished. God's plan is to reveal Christ into you, to make Christ your life and your everything, to regenerate and transform you to be a part of Christ, a member of Christ.

At one time Saul was fully occupied and zealous for the Jewish religion. The Jewish religion was the best religion because it was ordained and set up by God Himself. But that was not God's eternal plan. This young man Saul was zealous for that religion. His very life was for that religion, and we saw that he was breathing out something for that religion. But suddenly the Lord intervened to reveal His Son, Christ, into this active young man. He was busy with outward religious matters, yet God revealed His Son inwardly into him.

In Philippians 3 Paul mentions all of his attainments in the flesh in the Jewish religion (vv. 4-6). He was a Hebrew of the Hebrews and he was zealous for the law of Moses and the Jewish religion, but in 3:7 he says, "But what things were gains to me, these I have counted loss on account of

Christ." All the different gains were counted as one loss by
Paul because they all issued in one thing, that is, the loss of
Christ, as indicated by "on account of Christ." All the things
which were once gains to Paul hindered him and held him
back from participating in and enjoying Christ. Hence, on
account of Christ, all the gains were a loss to him.

Paul continued to say, "But surely I count also all things
to be loss on account of the excellency of the knowledge of
Christ Jesus my Lord, on account of whom I have suffered the
loss of all things and count them refuse that I may gain
Christ" (3:8). Paul counted as loss on account of Christ not
only the things of his former religion listed in verses 5 and 6,
but all other things as well. The word "refuse" in this verse
means dregs, rubbish, filth, what is thrown to the dogs;
hence, dog food, dung. There is no comparison between such
things and Christ. After Paul began to know Christ and
after he began to pursue Christ, he viewed all other things
as something rotten, dirty, corrupted, something thrown to
the dogs. The real food and the pure food for us is Christ
Himself. All things other than Christ are dung, are rotten,
corrupted, dirty, and are only good for the dogs.

Furthermore, Paul said that he counted all things refuse
that he might gain Christ and be found in Him (vv. 8-9). For
God to reveal Christ into you is one aspect. The other aspect
is that you will be found in Christ. Then Christ is in you,
and you are in Christ. No one can exhaust the meaning
of these two little phrases—Christ in me and I in Christ.
This simply means that you and Christ are one. Because you
are mingled, blended with Christ as one, when people persecute you they are persecuting Christ. Paul wanted to be found
in Christ, not having his own righteousness which is of the law,
but that which is through the faith of Christ, the righteousness which is of God based on faith (3:9). Our righteousness
is as filthy rags (Isa. 64:6). Paul wanted to live not in his
own righteousness but in the righteousness of God, and to be
found in such a transcendent condition, expressing God by
living Christ, not by keeping the law. To have the righteousness which is through the faith of Christ means through the
union with Christ, through the identification with Christ,

through the oneness with Christ. This is "the righteousness which is of God based on faith." Then Paul says, "To know Him and the power of His resurrection and the fellowship of His sufferings, being conformed to His death" (3:10). Paul had known Christ already but here he uses the present tense—that I may know Him. Paul wanted to experience Christ in the full knowledge of Him. He first received the revelation of Christ, and then sought for the experience of Christ—to know and enjoy Christ in an experiential way.

God's plan is to have Christ as our life and to have Christ as our image or our form. First, God put Christ into you as your life that you may live by Him, and second, God put you into Christ. Christ is the form, the mold, and you are like a piece of dough. The dough needs to be conformed to the mold. Christ is the life within and the mold without. Now we have to be conformed to Christ. After the dough is put into the mold, it is beaten to conform it to the mold and then put into the oven. If the dough could speak, it might say that this is not something good, yet we realize that for the dough to be conformed to the image of the mold it must pass through this process. In like manner, we have to be conformed to the death of Christ. By the fellowship of His sufferings, we will be conformed to His death and by this conformity we will be transformed into the same image as Christ; we will be made thoroughly one with Christ. This is God's plan.

What we have been fellowshipping is the kernel of the sixty-six books of the Bible. When we eat a peanut we do not care for the shell but for the kernel. The kernel of the Bible is that Christ has been revealed into us as life and that we live, have our being, and exist by Christ as the divine life. On the other hand, God put us into Christ with the desire that we would be conformed to the image of His Son (Rom. 8:29), that we might be transformed into the image of Christ to be thoroughly one with Christ. This is the center of the Bible and this is God's plan. This is the way God will build us together. Christ is in us, and we are in Him. Through regeneration, sanctification, transformation, and conformation we will be built up together as a living Body to contain and express Christ for His glory and our glorification.

We have to realize that the entire universe is for God's plan. Many philosophers and scientists have spent much time to find out the meaning of the universe, but very few of them know the real meaning of human life. The center of the universe is Christ in you and you in Christ. The real meaning of human life is Christ as your life with a view that you will be conformed to His image. The heavens and the earth with so many items are the background for the beautiful picture of God's plan. Praise the Lord that we are in His plan! It pleased God to reveal His Son in me, and I have to know Him, His resurrection power, and the fellowship of His sufferings. I need to be conformed to His death, transformed into His image that I might be built up with others as a living Body. Thus, in the whole universe there will be a universal Christ as the Head in the heavens and as the Body on this earth.

GOING ALONG WITH THE LORD
TO CARRY OUT HIS PLAN

One day I was brought to know the Lord. I do not understand why there was the inclination, the tendency, that I had to believe in Jesus. My countrymen told me that being a Christian would mean receiving a foreign religion, but I still had to receive Christ as my Savior. From that day, I tried many times to "divorce" Him, but He would not let me go. Something within me, on the one hand, has been comforting me all the time, yet on the other hand, has been bothering and troubling. Many times when I wanted to do something, the Lord within me did not want to do it, so there was a struggle between us. Many things within my being were contradicting Him. By His mercy, I am still here loving Him. I have been preserved not by mere teachings, but by the living Christ within me.

We need to thank the Lord and praise Him that we have Christ within us. Under His sovereignty you have received Him. You cannot give Him up or divorce Him because He is in you. You could "kick against the goads" until the end of your life, but when that day comes, you will still say with tears, "Lord, forgive me." I have seen some cases like this. Once the Lord has visited you and has been merciful to you,

you can never give Him up. You did not choose Him, but He chose you (John 15:16a). Your salvation is of Him, not of yourself. You may want to divorce Him, but He would not divorce you. The only thing you can do is to kick against the goads, but eventually you will recognize that He is the Lord and that you belong to Him. By that time, however, it may be too late—not too late for your salvation because you have been saved once for all for eternity—but too late for Him to work out something of His plan with you and through you.

It is better for you to make a decision today that you would go along with the Lord and allow Him to have the "freeway," the "expressway," to go on through you and with you. You have to offer yourself, to consecrate yourself, to give yourself to the Lord. You need to tell Him, "Lord, I am just a little creature in Your hands, and I know that You are the Lord. I thank You that You have dispensed Yourself into me as my life and that You desire to be everything to me. I want to hand myself over to You and go along with You for the carrying out of Your plan." If you do this, you will be the most blessed person on earth. You will be a part of God's plan to reveal Christ in you that you might be conformed to His image to be a member of His Body with a view that in this whole universe God will have a universal man with Christ as the Head in the heavens and with His believers as the members formed together as a Body on this earth to express Christ and to glorify God. This is God's plan with Christ as the center.

CHRIST VERSUS RELIGION

This young man Saul was born into and raised in the Jewish religion (Acts 22:3; 26:4-5). Saul was a religious person not just by teaching or training but by birth. Many of us were also religious people. We were born into and raised in Christianity. We were religious by birth. You may feel that it is good to be born into and raised in religion. It seems better than being born into and raised in a sinful environment. But we have to realize that religion does not help people to fulfill, to carry out, God's plan. Religion is even something against God's plan; it may be good but it is something other than Christ. It is hard for some people to really know Christ because they are so religious. They may know the doctrines, teachings, forms, rituals, and regulations, but they do not know the living Christ Himself.

In 1933 I was invited to speak in a chapel at a university in mainland China. Most of the audience were Christians, but they did not have the assurance that they had been saved. I had the burden to raise the question—"Do you have the assurance that you have been saved?" While I was speaking, a certain pastor sitting in the back was shaking his head in disagreement with what I was saying. This pastor might have contended for salvation by grace, but if you asked him if he had been saved, he would have responded, "Who can know today whether or not he has been saved?" This pastor might have had the doctrine of salvation by grace, but he did not have Christ Himself. It is possible to be involved in Christianity and yet not have Christ. You may have the forms and the regulations and yet not have Christ.

I was born into Christianity in mainland China. Before I was born again, I would contend with the Buddhist monks whenever they said something bad about Christianity. I fought for Christianity, yet I had not repented, prayed, and accepted Christ as my Savior. I had Christianity, but I did not have Christ. I had the religious forms, but I did not have Christ. I had the doctrines, the teachings, but I did not have Christ.

We need to look at today's situation in the light of this fellowship. Many Christians are involved in Christianity as a religion with forms, regulations, and teachings, yet they possess very little of Christ Himself. Many people are born into Christianity and have been raised in Christianity, but they do not know Christ. They need the Lord to intervene in their situation so that Christ can be revealed into them. Saul was born in Judaism, into the best religion, yet he needed a second birth. He needed to be regenerated, to be born again with the divine life.

You may say that you have already been born again, that you have already been regenerated. Praise the Lord for this! But do you realize that you have to go on to live not according to your first birth but according to your second birth? You should live not by the life from your first birth, but by the life from your second birth. The Christian life is not a matter of religion, teachings, doctrines, forms, or regulations, but simply a matter of Christ Himself. You have to receive Christ as life, you have to deal with Him as the unique Lord in this universe, and you have to live in Him to be conformed to His image. You need the revelation Saul had on the way to Damascus.

Before Saul was met by Christ on the way to Damascus, he was, no doubt, a brilliant, religious, zealous, and strong young man. But when Christ intervened, this strong man became weak. This young man was awfully strong. He was taking the lead to persecute the believers, to devastate the church, yet after he was met by the Lord he became very weak. After Saul fell and rose from the ground, he had become blind and needed someone to lead him by the hand (Acts 9:8). This was the Lord's dealing with Saul. Before this he would have considered himself marvelously knowledgeable, knowing all things concerning man and God. Now the Lord made him blind so that he could see nothing until the Lord opened his eyes, especially his inner eyes, and commissioned him to open the eyes of others (26:18).

After three days, the Lord sent a member of the Body of Christ by the name of Ananias to come and lay hands on Saul (9:10-19). When Ananias laid hands on Saul and spoke to him, the Word tells us that "there fell from his eyes something like scales, and he received his sight" (v. 18). Then his inner eyes were opened and he could see something of the Lord, something spiritual. This was a great transfer, a great turning point. Thus, Saul of Tarsus became a factor to turn the age. He was transformed, transferred, and turned, so he could transfer the age, so he could turn the age.

We need to look at Saul and compare ourselves with him. This picture of Saul should show us that what we need is not religion with its forms, teachings, and knowledge, but the realization of the living Christ who is the center of God's eternal plan. Day by day you have Him within you, yet you need more and more vision and revelation concerning Him. You have to pursue Him. You have to know Him more and more and let Him have more ground within you. Do not pay your attention to religion, to the many activities in Christianity, or to your outward doings. These are things in religion, having nothing to do with God's plan. What you need is the inward knowledge of Christ, the inner experience of Christ. What you need is to open yourself, to offer yourself, to give yourself to the Lord and let Him have the ground to impart Himself into you day by day. Let Him work Himself into you and through you to fulfill God's eternal plan.

We all need to have some time with the Lord to pray: "By Your mercy, Lord, I now know the meaning of God's plan and what the center of this plan is. Here I am, Lord, fully open to You and ready to be taken by You, to be possessed by You. Grant me Your mercy that I may know how to live by You, how to walk in You, and how to go along with You that You might have the free way and the full ground to work Yourself into me and to work out through me." Then you will be one of the most blessed persons in this age, and you will be one who will turn the age. You will be a person who will transfer many others into God's eternal plan.

CHAPTER THREE

SAUL'S LIFE AND CONVERSION

As Christians we need to know God's eternal plan in this universe, God's plan for His unique purpose and desire. We should have a time with the Lord about this matter. Merely to understand the points of fellowship in this book in your mind is not good enough. You need some impression in your spirit before the Lord. You may even be clear about God's plan, yet you should digest what you understand by praying. Then something will be impressed into your spirit, and what you understand will be a real strengthening, a real power, a real force within you. May we all pray about and with the truths and the fellowship contained in this book. In the previous chapter we saw Saul's birth and religion. In this chapter we want to go on to see his life and his conversion. Saul was born and raised up in Judaism and he spontaneously had a life fully according to that religion. His life before his conversion was one hundred percent according to his religion. He lived for and by what he believed.

RELIGION AND TRADITION VERSUS
CHRIST AND THE REVELATION OF CHRIST

Galatians 1:13 says, "For you have heard of my manner of life formerly in Judaism, that I persecuted the church of God excessively and ravaged it." Saul persecuted the church of God, not because he was sinful but because he was religious. He was so zealous for his religion that he persecuted the church of God because the church of God was something different from his religion. In Galatians 1:14-16a Paul continues, "And I advanced in Judaism beyond many contemporaries in my race, being more exceedingly zealous of the traditions of

my fathers. But when it pleased God, who set me apart
from my mother's womb and called me through His grace,
to reveal His Son in me." Saul made progress in his religion
beyond his contemporaries and he was zealous for the traditions of his fathers, but it pleased God to reveal His Son in
Saul.

In the passage we have just read there are four important
items: religion, tradition, Christ, and the revelation of Christ.
Saul was involved in the best religion, the Jewish religion, a
religion ordained by God with good traditions, many of which
were according to the teachings of the Old Testament. Yet this
religion with so many traditions was something contradicting
with Christ and with the revelation of Christ. If you read this
portion of Scripture carefully, you will realize the difference
between Christ and religion and between the revelation of
Christ and the traditions of religion. Religion is versus Christ
and the traditions are versus the revelation of Christ.

Many of us may be like that young man Saul. He was born
in a religion and we also were born in a religion. In this religion we have many traditions. I was born into Christianity,
and in today's Christianity there are many traditions. Are
you a Christian today living, walking, working, and serving
the Lord according to the traditions of Christianity or according to the revelation of Christ, the Son of the living God? Are
you dealing with a formed, organized religion or are you dealing with a living Person? Are you dealing with the living
Christ, the Son of the living God?

Saul was a brilliant man with a superior makeup. From
the human point of view he was not so sinful but rather good
and religious. Yet he was dealing with a religion, not with
the living Christ. He was serving Christ according to the
tradition of his fathers, not according to the living revelation
of the Holy Spirit. We have to realize even today that there is
the possibility that people could serve God by dealing with a
religion according to many traditions, not by dealing with the
living Christ and not according to the living revelation of the
Holy Spirit. I do not have any intention to help others to be
religious. On the contrary, I would do my best to tear down all
the religious matters in you. I do pray to the Lord that He

would open your eyes to give you a turning point, that you could turn from a religion to a living Person—Christ—and turn from the traditions to the revelation of Christ. This young man's life before his conversion was apparently not evil but good and religious, yet he needed Christ to be revealed in him.

In Philippians 3 Paul speaks of all that he was and had in his natural being: "Circumcised the eighth day; of the race of Israel, of the tribe of Benjamin, a Hebrew of Hebrews; as to the law, a Pharisee; as to zeal, persecuting the church; as to the righteousness which is in the law, become blameless. But what things were gains to me, these I have counted loss on account of Christ" (vv. 5-7). In these verses are the life of this man before his conversion and his attitude after his conversion. What was this young man converted from? We think a man is always converted from sin to God. We need some conversion because we are sinful and have fallen away from God. According to the Scriptures, however, Saul was converted from religion to Christ. From the point of view of God, Saul's persecuting of the church was something sinful, yet from the human point of view, from the religious point of view, he was not sinful but may have been appreciated, admired, and praised by many religious persons. Paul was converted from religion to Christ, not merely from sin to God.

In the past I met a number of people who were born Christians, but not converted Christians, not reborn Christians. They were born and raised up in Christianity and even lived for Christianity. They were good people and they were very religious. Many of them were doing a religious work, yet they did not know Christ in a living, experiential way. They had a religion, but they did not have life. They had Christianity, but they did not have Christ Himself. They were engaged in many activities, programs, and works, but they did not have the inner life with the inner impact. Look at today's Christianity and ask yourself what the percentage of activities, programs, and outward works is and what the percentage of inward life is. Christ as the living One should be realized, experienced, enjoyed, applied, and appreciated by us all the time.

CONVERTED FROM EVERYTHING TO CHRIST HIMSELF

You may have been regenerated, but maybe even today you need a real, practical conversion from the traditional things, from the religious things, unto the living Christ. A person can only be regenerated once. But in my experience I can testify that I have had a number of conversions. Regeneration is once for all, but conversion, to have some change in your life, is not just once for all.

I was born in Christianity, and I was taught and raised up in Christianity. But when I was nineteen years old, I was regenerated, and that was my first conversion. A real change in life transpired inwardly. Not long after I had been regenerated, I began to meet with a group of Christians who paid much attention to the teachings, to the knowledge of the Bible. I stayed with them for seven and a half years. After those seven and a half years, one day the Lord gave me another conversion, another change. He opened my eyes to see that the Christian life is not a matter of merely dealing with the knowledge of the Bible or with doctrine, but a matter of dealing with Christ as the living One. That brought about a great change in my life. I was so clear that to be a Christian is not a matter of knowledge, not a matter of just studying the Bible in letters, in black and white, but a matter of dealing with the living Christ as your life.

With this realization I then began to serve the Lord. In our experience, many times we get the grace and the deliverance, but after a while we drift away. When you are serving the Lord it is easy to be tempted to pay attention to the work, not to pay attention to the flow of life and to the work that proceeds out of this flow. After I learned how to experience Christ as life and how to deal with this living Christ, the Lord really gave me the burden for the work. I worked diligently, heartily, and even fruitfully. I worked and worked day and night, day after day. But one day the Lord intervened and stopped me from the work. It would have been rather hard for anyone to keep me away from the work, but the Lord intervened and put me into a position where it was absolutely impossible for me to work. This was another conversion experience for me. I absolutely had no ability to work due to a serious illness I contracted. I was kept absolutely away from the work by the Lord for nearly two and a half years. In that time I was converted from the work to the Lord Himself.

At the beginning of that time, I was thinking that maybe I was wrong in something, so I did my best to confess whatever I thought was wrong to the Lord. Eventually the Lord showed me that the problem with me was that I paid much more attention to the work than to the Lord Himself. I was converted at that time not from sin to God, but from the work to Christ Himself. Before that time the work for the Lord was my life. No one could stop me from working for the Lord. You could have taken away many things from me without my being concerned. But I would not have tolerated even a little bit of the Lord's work being taken from me. Now I still work for the Lord, but the work by itself is not preeminent to me. The most important thing is the living Lord Himself. We should labor in the Lord, but our labor should not be something between us and the living Lord.

It may be quite possible that there are many good things between you and the Lord. It is possible to have something in religion, some work, some program, or some activity in Christianity to take the place of Christ in your life. We need a conversion not necessarily from anything sinful or evil, but from good things, from religious things, from substitutes for Christ Himself, which prevent Him from occupying, filling, saturating, permeating, and possessing our entire inward being.

We need to ask ourselves what we are seeking. Today's religious system with its traditions is a big problem to many Christians. On the one hand, Christianity seemingly brings people to Christ. But on the other hand, it also becomes a barrier, a hindrance, keeping people from the inner experience and enjoyment of Christ. The many Christian activities, Christian works, and Christian programs on the one hand bring people to Christ, but on the other hand keep people from Christ. They bring people to Christ up to a certain point. Then they become a barrier, a limitation, a hindrance. Even the desire to be spiritual can become something that takes the ground in our being to replace Christ Himself. I have seen some who take care of being "spiritual" more than the Lord Himself. We need many conversions from everything other than the living Christ Himself.

Another conversion that I experienced was related to my love for the study of the Word. After I was saved, I loved to study the Word. The Word was so sweet to me, just like honey. When I was a young believer, I would take the Bible to bed with me so I could look at it as soon as I awoke in the morning. Eventually, this love to study the Word became something taking the ground of Christ in my life. I loved the study of the Word much more than Christ Himself. Many times I had the anointing and the burden to pray, but because I was addicted to the study of the Word, I would not give up this study to pray. Eventually and sovereignly, the Lord intervened and now I dare not study the Word in that way. I was also very fond of teaching the Scriptures. I loved to interpret and expound the Scriptures. Now I have to take care of the limitation within me whenever I give a message. Even this matter can become something between you and the Lord Himself. Now I am careful not to go beyond what the Lord is speaking in me (2 Cor. 13:3) and what He needs me to speak.

There could be many things in our life which take the place of the Lord Himself. My burden is to fellowship with you and help you to realize that God's plan is to work Christ Himself into you (Gal. 1:16; 2:20; 4:19). This is God's goal, His ultimate intention. Do not think God's intention is to make you merely spiritual. Even spirituality might become something in you that is in contradiction to God's plan. The work for the Lord, the activities in Christianity, the progress for the gospel, and so many other good things could possibly be a hindrance, a substitute for Christ. You need to be converted all the time from something other than Christ to Christ Himself. Whenever anything becomes a hindrance between you and Christ, you have to be converted from that to Christ Himself.

I knew some sisters who loved to fellowship with other sisters. This kind of fellowship eventually became a hindrance between them and the Lord and took the place of the Lord in their lives. They loved this kind of fellowship more than Christ Himself. With these sisters there was the need to be converted, not from anything sinful but from this good fellowship to Christ Himself. You have to consider whether or not something in your life is taking the place of Christ. Is something in your life more important than Christ Himself? If so, you have to be converted from this very thing to Christ. Regeneration is a conversion, but a conversion to us Christians is not just once for all. We need many conversions. Anything, no matter how good it might be, can become a hindrance, a barrier between you and Christ, taking the place of Christ in your life and substituting Christ in your life. May we all be converted from everything other than Christ to the living Person of Christ Himself.

GOD'S DESIRE FOR US TO BE ONE WITH CHRIST, FILLED WITH CHRIST, AND OCCUPIED BY CHRIST TO LIVE CHRIST

We have to see what God's plan is. Do you think God's plan is to make you so zealous, religious, and spiritual? To be religious is much better than being sinful. To be zealous for Christianity is really better than being worldly, and to be spiritual is really better than being carnal. Yet you have to realize that even being spiritual could be a barrier between you and Christ and could be a substitute of Christ to you. One young man may be very worldly. He may love the world, seek the worldly things, and pursue after the world. Another young man may be very religious and may have given up the world totally. But what is the difference between these two young men as far as Christ is concerned? There may be no difference. In the worldly young man we cannot see Christ, and in this religious young man we can neither see anything of Christ.

We can use two bottles as an illustration. The purpose of these bottles is to contain some kind of beverage. One bottle may be dirty and the other may be clean, but the bottles were not made merely to be clean. They were made to be filled with a certain beverage. In like manner, God does not merely desire to have many "clean people." What God wants to have is many people filled with Christ. He does not want religious people but Christians. A Christian is a Christ-man, a man filled with Christ, a man mingled with Christ, a man lost in Christ. All over the world, it is relatively easy to meet Christians, but it is not so easy to meet some Christians who are filled with Christ and whose goal is Christ Himself. It is possible to meet many working Christians, religious Christians, and active Christians who act for Christ, yet it is not so easy to meet some Christians who are one with Christ, filled with Christ, and occupied solely by Christ.

I have the impression that many may be working for a religious system just like Saul of Tarsus worked for Judaism. You may be working for religion and have nothing to do with Christ. I hope that the Lord has opened our eyes to see that God's plan is to reveal His Son in us so that we can be conformed to the image of His Son. God's intention and God's plan is not for us to be religious, good, spiritual, or knowledgeable of the Scriptures, but God's plan is for us to be filled with Christ, to be occupied, possessed, saturated, permeated, blended, and mingled with Christ. This is why Paul tells us in Philippians 3:7-8, "But what things were gains to me, these I have counted loss on account of Christ. But surely I count also all things to be loss on account of the excellency of the knowledge of Christ Jesus my Lord, on account of whom I have suffered the loss of all things and count them refuse that I may gain Christ." Paul was brought to the realization that the only gain in the universe was Christ Himself. To him Christ was the one reality of all. Nothing was real to him but Christ.

In Philippians 3:3 Paul says, "For we are the circumcision, who serve by the Spirit of God and boast in Christ Jesus, and have no confidence in the flesh." The phrase "serve by the Spirit of God" can also be rendered "worship God in the spirit" (KJV). This is similar to what the Lord Jesus said in John 4:24, that God is Spirit and those who worship Him must worship Him in spirit. Philippians 3:3 also tells us that Paul did not boast in his religion, in his purity, in his cleanness, or in his religious activity. He boasted in Christ Jesus. We should worship God in the spirit and boast in Christ as the reality. Nothing other than Christ should be important to us or should be real to us. Our lives need to be occupied solely with Christ Himself.

We all have to pay the price in this matter. Many things can creep in, even good things other than Christ, to take the place of Christ in the life of Christians. It is not only the world and sin that can hinder us from seeking Christ, that can keep us away from Christ. Even good things, religious things, and even things concerning Christ can hinder us from seeking and being occupied with Christ Himself. Therefore, we have to learn the lesson always to count everything as a loss on account of Christ. The things the apostle Paul counted as loss were not bad things. All the things he counted as loss were good things, but those things were not Christ Himself. Even many Christians are seeking spiritual gifts, but the gifts can be substitutions of Christ. If we focus ourselves on Christ Himself to have the genuine experience of Christ, then any gift that we have will also be Christ Himself.

We must remember that God's plan is to work Christ into us, and we have to pay attention to Christ Himself, nothing else. We do not agree that anything would come into our life to take the place of Christ. We like to count everything as a loss on account of the excellency of the knowledge of Christ Jesus our Lord. Paul's desire was "to know Him and the power of His resurrection and the fellowship of His sufferings, being conformed to His death" (Phil. 3:10). Paul wanted to be mingled with Christ, to be transformed into Christ in order to become a real member of Christ. If you would seek and experience Christ in this way, you will have the power, the fruit, the spirituality, and everything which is good in the eyes of God. The reason for this is that everything which is good in the eyes of God must be something of Christ Himself. If you have Christ, you will have everything. As the chorus of *Hymns,* #513 says, "Everything is in Christ, and Christ is everything."

Paul's life was to live Christ (Phil. 1:21a). To him to live was Christ, not the law nor circumcision. He would not live the law but Christ, not be found in the law but in Christ (3:9).

Christ was not only his life within but also his living without. He lived Christ because Christ lived in him (Gal. 2:20). He was one with Christ both in life and in living. He and Christ, they two, had one life and one living. They lived together as one person. Christ lived within him as his life, and he lived Christ without as his living. The normal experience of Christ is to live Him, and to live Him is to magnify Him always, regardless of the circumstances.

God's plan is to work Christ into us, so throughout our life we need many conversions. Whenever there is something in your life substituting Christ, you need a conversion from that very thing to Christ Himself. We should always keep ourselves in direct contact with Christ. Then we will be one with Christ in reality.

CHAPTER FOUR

SAUL'S VISION AND COMMISSION

Thus far, we have seen God's plan and Saul's birth, religion, life, and conversion. Now we want to see Saul's vision and commission. Acts 26:17-18 says, "Taking you out from the people and from the Gentiles, to whom I send you, to open their eyes, to turn them from darkness to light and from the authority of Satan to God, that they may receive forgiveness of sins and an inheritance among those who have been sanctified by faith in Me." These verses show us the five items of Saul's commission: (1) to open their eyes; (2) to turn them from darkness to light; (3) to turn them from the authority of Satan to God; (4) that they may receive forgiveness of sins; (5) and that they may receive an inheritance among those who have been sanctified by faith in the Lord Jesus.

The word inheritance in verse 18 may also be translated into lot or portion. This Greek word is also used in Colossians 1:12 which says, "Giving thanks to the Father, who has qualified you for a share of the portion of the saints in the light." The portion of the saints in Colossians 1:12 is the portion of those who have been sanctified by faith in the Lord in Acts 26:18. Colossians 1:12 refers to the portion of the saints and Acts 26:18 refers to the portion among those who have been sanctified. The saints are the persons who have been sanctified by God. The portion of the saints is Christ Himself. The entire book of Colossians deals with the fact that God gave the all-inclusive Christ to us as our portion. All the treasures of wisdom and knowledge are hidden in this all-inclusive Person (Col. 2:3), and all the fullness of the Godhead dwells in

Him bodily (v. 9). Christ has been given to us as a divine portion allotted to us by God.

THE DIVINE COMMISSION
ACCORDING TO THE HEAVENLY VISION

In Acts 26:19 Paul told King Agrippa that he "was not disobedient to the heavenly vision." Paul could not be disobedient to what he had seen. His commission was according to his vision. What you are going to do for the Lord must be according to what you have seen of the Lord. Because you have seen something of the Lord, you have to do something for the Lord according to what you have seen. Thus, the commission is according to the vision, and the vision creates the commission.

If we have really seen God's plan and have been really converted from the things other than Christ to Christ Himself, what we have seen and experienced will produce or create a commission for us. This vision will cause us to act, to work for Christ, to serve Christ, according to what we have seen of Him. If I have really seen that Christ is everything, that He is my life, my experience, and the meaning and center of my life, there will be no need for the responsible ones of the church to come to tell me that I have to do something for the Lord as a member of the church. Once you have seen a vision of God's plan and have been converted from everything to Christ Himself, there will be something within you energizing you to carry out God's plan. Because you have experienced something of Christ and have seen something of Christ, no one can stop you from working together with the Lord and from ministering something of Christ to others. There will be something within you energizing you to contact people.

When we contact other believers, we will fellowship with them about the Christ whom we know. Our commission and ministry come out of the heavenly vision. The more that you contact the Lord in prayer, the more you will be burdened for so many unbelievers. As a result of your inward burden for those who do not know Christ, who do not have Christ, it will be easy for you to preach the gospel. Preaching the gospel will not merely be an outward work for you, but something being worked out from within you. Then when you contact people, you are not going to bring them some doctrines, forms, regulations, or creeds. You are not bringing a religion to them, but you are bringing the living person of Christ to them. Your burden is to impart Christ to them.

It may be that you would fellowship with another Christian brother about Christ being in the believers (Col. 1:27; 2 Cor. 13:5). He may say that he knows this. Then you can ask him, "What is your experience of Christ as life?" If you are so living in the spirit, what you say to him will impart Christ and will have an impact. The Holy Spirit will honor what you say. Within one or two minutes you can make a real impression on this brother. After his contact with you, he may wonder for days what it means to have Christ within him. He will desire to get back in touch with you to find out what it means to have Christ within him. He will be so open and you will be able to minister Christ into him. You are going to bring Christ to people, and this commission depends on your seeing. Because you have experienced the Lord and seen Him, you have something within you energizing and operating to impel you to serve the Lord in ministering Him to others.

THE CONTENTS OF OUR COMMISSION

The five points of Paul's commission in Acts 26:18 are all-inclusive. First, we need to open others' eyes. Whenever you talk with people it should open their eyes. This is something different from merely teaching someone. This is the way to realize whether or not a ministry is living. If a ministry is living, it must open people's eyes. A man may be quite learned, possessing a high degree, but when he speaks he does not open the eyes of people. On the other hand, another brother may be unskilled in utterance and even stammering in his speaking, but because of his vision he can open people's eyes. When you have the heavenly vision, you will open others' eyes even if you speak without eloquence. You may be dull in utterance, but skilled in opening people's eyes. Saul as a young man in God's plan had his eyes opened, so he knew how to open the inner eyes of others. Whether or not your word, your ministry, could open other people's eyes depends upon how much you have seen and how much you have experienced.

What you speak should also turn people. Whoever listens to you speak should not be the same as he was before. You need to turn people from darkness to light and from the authority of Satan to God. Darkness is a sign of sin and death; light, a sign of righteousness and life (John 1:4; 8:12). The authority of Satan is Satan's kingdom (Matt. 12:26 and note) which belongs to darkness. On the positive side, people have to be helped to realize the real forgiveness of sins from God, and also they need to receive Christ, the Son of God, as their portion.

These five points in Acts 26:18 must be the very contents of our commission which comes from a living vision of Christ, from the real experience of Christ. Because you are living under the heavenly vision, many times you will work unconsciously, and Christ will be ministered through you. You will have a surplus of Christ, and whenever you come to the meetings of the church you will exhibit Christ (see *Hymns,* #864). If we all would bring a surplus of Christ to the church meetings, Christ would be exhibited in a rich way. When people come into such a meeting they will see that we are weighty, living, and powerful. The Lord wants to recover Christ Himself to be realized by us as everything. Christ Himself is our knowledge, our teaching, our regulation, our form, our gifts, our power, our weight, and our riches. If you have Christ, you have everything. The Christian life is not a matter of religion, of teachings, of forms, of regulations, or of gifts, but a matter of Christ Himself.

If you would be faithful to the Lord, the Lord could work out something through you to accomplish His eternal plan. However, if you take the traditional way, the religious way, the organizational way, you cannot carry out God's plan. If you take the way of Christ, the living way (see Acts 9:2, note 2[1]; and 2 Pet. 2:2, note 2[2]), something wonderful will be worked out through you for the Lord. You may think that you do not have any gift or ability, but you will be a fruitful person bringing many able and gifted persons to the Lord. You will do this not merely by preaching or teaching but by a living contact with people, imparting Christ into them.

This young man, Saul of Tarsus, is a real example to us. It may be that in the entire Scriptures only the Lord Jesus as a man could exceed this man Saul, who was later called Paul. Paul even told us in 1 Timothy that he was a pattern to the believers (1:16). Saul was religious and natural, yet one day he received the heavenly vision and was converted from all things other than Christ to Christ Himself. From that day he became very useful in the hand of God and had a prevailing impact. The Lord was able to accomplish many wonderful things through him. This is the kind of person whom God can use today. May we all go to the Lord and pray, "Lord, here I am. I am open to You, to Your vision, to Your commission, and I am ready to pay any cost, any price. I want to count all things loss and count only Christ as gain. I am ready to be occupied, possessed, and filled by Christ." If we go to the Lord and spend some time with Him to receive the heavenly vision, we will have a living contact with Christ and be a living, functioning member of His living Body. Then we will be persons in God's plan.

ABOUT THE AUTHOR

Witness Lee was born in 1905 in northern China and raised in a Christian family. At age 19 he was fully captured for Christ and immediately consecrated himself to preach the gospel for the rest of his life. Early in his service, he met Watchman Nee, a renowned preacher, teacher, and writer. Witness Lee labored together with Watchman Nee under his direction. In 1934 Watchman Nee entrusted Witness Lee with the responsibility for his publication operation, called the Shanghai Gospel Bookroom.

Prior to the Communist takeover in 1949, Witness Lee was sent by Watchman Nee and his other co-workers to Taiwan to ensure that the things delivered to them by the Lord would not be lost. Watchman Nee instructed Witness Lee to continue the former's publishing operation abroad as the Taiwan Gospel Bookroom, which has been publicly recognized as the publisher of Watchman Nee's works outside China. Witness Lee's work in Taiwan manifested the Lord's abundant blessing. From a mere 350 believers, newly fled from the mainland, the churches in Taiwan grew to 20,000 in five years.

In 1962 Witness Lee felt led of the Lord to come to the United States, settling in California. During his 35 years of service in the U.S., he ministered in weekly meetings and weekend conferences, delivering several thousand spoken messages. Much of his speaking has since been published as over 400 titles. Many of these have been translated into over fourteen languages. He gave his last public conference in February 1997 at the age of 91.

He leaves behind a prolific presentation of the truth in the Bible. His major work, *Life-study of the Bible*, comprises over 25,000 pages of commentary on every book of the Bible from the perspective of the believers' enjoyment and experience of God's divine life in Christ through the Holy Spirit. Witness Lee was the chief editor of a new translation of the New Testament into Chinese called the Recovery Version and directed the translation of the same into English. The Recovery Version also appears in a number of other languages. He provided an extensive body of footnotes, outlines, and spiritual cross references. A radio broadcast of his messages can be heard on Christian radio stations in the United States. In 1965 Witness Lee founded Living Stream Ministry, a non-profit corporation, located in Anaheim, California, which officially presents his and Watchman Nee's ministry.

Witness Lee's ministry emphasizes the experience of Christ as life and the practical oneness of the believers as the Body of Christ. Stressing the importance of attending to both these matters, he led the churches under his care to grow in Christian life and function. He was unbending in his conviction that God's goal is not narrow sectarianism but the Body of Christ. In time, believers began to meet simply as the church in their localities in response to this conviction. In recent years a number of new churches have been raised up in Russia and in many eastern European countries.